NEFERTITI: THE MYSTERY QUEEN

BY BURNHAM HOLMES

A

Book

From
RAINTREE CHILDRENS BOOKS
Milwaukee • Toronto • Melbourne • London

Library of Congress Number: 77-10445

Art and Photo Credits

Cover photo, John Bennett Dobbins/Photo Trends
Photo on page 6, The Museum of Fine Arts, Boston
Photos on pages 10, 12, and 29, The Metropolitan Museum of Art
Photo on page 15, J. Alex Langley/dpi
Photo on page 16, Harry Burton/The Metropolitan Museum of Art
Photo on page 19, The Metropolitan Museum of Art, gift of
Edward S. Harkness, 1921
Photo on page 20, The Brooklyn Museum, Charles Edwin Wilbour Fund
Photo on page 25, Jeffrey Foxx/Woodfin Camp & Associates
Photo on page 26, The Metropolitan Museum of Art, gift of
J. Pierpont Morgan, 1917
Photo on page 30, Brian Brake/Photo Researchers, Inc.
Illustration on page 36, N.Y. Public Library Picture Collection
Photo on page 39, The Metropolitan Museum of Art, The Theodore M. Davis
Collection. Bequest of Theodore M. Davis, 1915.
Photo on page 43, Wide World Photos, Inc.
Photo on page 44, George Holton/Photo Researchers, Inc.
Photo on page 45, The Metropolitan Museum of Art, gift of Mr. and Mrs. Everit
Macy, 1923
Photo on page 47, The Metropolitan Museum of Art, Rogers Fund, 1925
All photo research for this book was provided by Roberta Guerette.
Every effort has been made to trace the ownership of all copyrighted material in
this book and to obtain permission for its use.

Library of Congress Cataloging in Publication Data

Holmes, Burnham, 1942-
  Nefertiti: the mystery queen.

  SUMMARY: The life of Nefertiti concentrating on the period
during which her husband, Amenhotep IV, struggled to change the
ancient forms of worship in Egypt from many gods to one, the sun
god.
  1. Egypt—History—To 332 B.C.—Juvenile literature. 2. Nefertiti,
Queen of Egypt, 14th cent. B.C.—Juvenile literature. 3. Amenhotep
IV, King of Egypt, 1388-1358 B.C.—Juvenile literature. [1. Nefertiti,
Queen of Egypt, 14th cent. B.C. 2. Queens. 3. Egypt—History—To
332 B.C.] I. Title.
DT87.45.H64   932'.01'0924 [B] [92]   77-10445
ISBN 0-8172-1056-3 lib. bdg.

Manufactured in the United States of America
ISBN 0-8172-1056-3

CONTENTS

Chapter 1

THE SEARCH BEGINS

The year was 1912. The setting was the ancient ruins of Tell el-Amarna in Middle Egypt. A group of German archeologists was digging to find the ancient city named Akhetaton.

Finding a stone tablet, the archeologists stopped to translate the picture writings on its face. The tablet told them they were presently in the workroom of Tuthmose, "the Chief Craftsman, Sculptor, and Favorite of the King." This room had been built more than 3,000 years ago!

Suddenly one of the archeologists struck something hard with his shovel. Perhaps the scientists were getting close to their ancient city.

5

The picture writings on stone tablets from Tell el-Amarna
describe much of what we know about the ancient Egyptians.

The other workers gathered around to scrape
the sand away. What they saw astonished them.
First a flesh-colored neck appeared. Then they
saw the face of a woman—her eyes of rock crys-
tal stared up at them. On her head was a blue
crown. The crown was decorated with an Egyptian cobra—the symbol of Egyptian royalty.

6

The German scientists soon learned that they had made one of the most important discoveries of their time. The stone head they had uncovered was indeed a royal one. It was the face of Nefertiti, ancient Egypt's mystery queen. Their find raised many questions all over the world. Little if anything was known about this beautiful queen. No one was sure she ever really lived at all! She lived and died quite mysteriously. Now, perhaps, more of her secrets would be revealed. Who was Queen Nefertiti? When did she live? Why was she so important and yet so mysterious? What really happened to her?

Nefertiti's name never appeared in official Egyptian records. It was thought she lived only in Egyptian stories. Since the stone head was found, Egyptian experts tried to put together the puzzle of her life.

Here is Nefertiti's story—the story of an Egyptian queen. It is told as if she were telling it today.

Chapter 2

NEFERTITI SPEAKS

I lived during a good age for my country, more than 3,000 years ago.

We had strong leaders and strong priests. Our armies and navies won wars with foreign lands. Egypt overflowed with gold. Our artists built huge, beautiful temples for the gods. Great tombs honored our dead kings and their families. It seemed as if Egypt ruled the world. At least as much of the world as we knew.

I was born in 1384 B.C. in the royal city of Thebes. My name, Nefertiti, means "the Beautiful One Has Come." My mother, Tiy, was the Royal Nurse for the family of King Amenhotep

III and Queen Tiy. But my mother was more than just their nurse. She and the Queen were very close friends. Both of them came from poor families. (As you have probably noticed, my mother's name was the same as the Queen's. She did this to honor the Queen.)

My father's name was Aye. Although few have heard of him, Aye was a very important person in the history of ancient Egypt.

My father started out simply enough. He had no wealth or family title. He searched for a career and decided to become a scribe, a writer for the King's important records. Scribes were very important in our day because few people could read or write. It took my father years to learn *hieroglyphics*—a system of pictures that stood for words in ancient Egypt.

When he finished his schooling, my father went to work for King Amenhotep III. Aye was very good at his work and soon became the chief scribe. This allowed him to sit in on every important decision the King made.

Aye was smart and hardworking. It wasn't long before Amenhotep III appointed him Grand Vizier (which was like a minister of state).

*My father-in-law, Amenhotep III, is pictured in a wall painting
with his mother.*

My father was no longer just writing down the King's laws, he was *making* them!

Our family (which now included my younger sister, Nezemmut) lived near the palace of the King. My childhood was spent playing in and around the royal palace and by the banks of the Nile with my best friend, Amenhotep. He was the King's son.

Amenhotep was a year older than I and had the same name as his father. He was the oldest son and would someday be the king. As you might imagine, this was a big responsibility even when he was a young prince. Not that he didn't like to play. He enjoyed watching a new litter of royal kittens or trying to spear the quick, darting bolti fish as much as I did. But as time passed, he spent more time with his father and less with me. Amenhotep had much to learn if he was to be a good king in the future.

In addition to being the King's scribe and Grand Vizier, my father was also the Commander of Horse. This meant that he was in charge of all the King's chariots. The Commander of Horse was saluted by those entering the palace. The visitors would first salute the

Amenhotep and I enjoyed long hours together hunting wild birds and spearing bolti fish.

King and Queen, then the Commander and his chariots and horses.

Oh yes, before I forget, my father was also the Prince's tutor. There was no one in the kingdom as able to give him a good education as my father. And Amenhotep was a good student. He was always asking questions. As far as I know, he always received an answer.

Chapter 3

GROOMED TO BE QUEEN

I was very young when the Queen and my mother realized that I might very well marry Prince Amenhotep. We loved each other as brother and sister. So, although I didn't receive much formal education (certainly not like the Prince's), I was groomed to be the future queen.

When I put away my playthings for the last time, there were many women of the court to wait on me. They would bathe me, apply make-up, and dress me for the day. This took many hours. The Egyptians thought women should always look beautiful. Everyone wanted to make sure that I was as beautiful as the meaning of my name.

During this time, I could go anywhere, even into the busy streets of Thebes. Unlike the old days, Egyptian women were now allowed to appear alone in public, to own property, and to be on an equal basis with men. King Amenhotep III had a lot to do with these new rights of women. I'm glad his son also felt the same way. And why not? Two of the most important people in his life were women, Queen Tiy and I!

Thebes, the royal city where we lived, was beautiful. But King Amenhotep III wanted to make it even more beautiful. He needed someone to plan and carry out the many building projects he had in mind. And the perfect man to do this was my father. Aye had studied geometry and science to become a scribe and was always interested in designing and building. Aye's most impressive buildings were the *Colossi of Memnon*, the *Temple of Luxor*, and the burial tomb called *Kom el Haitan*.

The Colossi of Memnon were statues of Amenhotep III and Queen Tiy carved of stone and over 50 feet high. We had hundreds of gods in those days, and the Temple of Luxor was built to honor the god of our city—the sun god Amon. Not only was the Temple of Luxor holy, it was also beautiful. It was connected to Queen Tiy's palace by a garden that was over a mile long and full of trees and flowers.

Kom el Haitan was located in the Valley of the Kings, where many kings of the past were buried. The building of burial tombs began during a king's lifetime. Death was a very important event for us. We loved life and wanted to enjoy it forever. We believed we could live again in a new life after death. To protect our treasures and bodies, we had great tombs built. The tombs of our most important kings were built

My father, Aye, was proud of the Temple of Luxor, built to honor the sun-god Amon.

Both Amenhotep III and Queen Tiy had giant tombs built in the Valley of the Kings.

into the Pyramids. Some of these giant stone triangle-shaped buildings remain standing even today.

Not only were the tombs built to last, but they were supplied with everything the king and his royal family would need in the other world. There were food, wine, and treasures such as you've never seen.

Many of my people spent all their lives in "the city of the dead." Their job was to prepare the royal bodies for the new life after death. This was not an easy job. It took great skill and training. The vital organs were removed from the body. These organs were placed in large decorated jars. Carved stones in the shape of beetles were put into the body in place of the organs. The stones had holy writings on them. The bodies were then drained, treated with chemicals, and wrapped in cloth. All this was done to preserve the bodies for all time. Some of our mummies are still in perfect shape and can be seen in modern museums—*thousands of years after death.*

After the long burial process, the dead were ready to meet the god *Osiris.* The person who had led a good life and done good works could join Osiris and live forever.

Chapter 4

THE BEGINNING

In 1372 B.C., the health of Amenhotep III was beginning to fail. He asked his 13-year-old son to rule with him. In ancient Egypt, children had to grow up quickly. When we were in our early teens, we were looked upon as adults.

Young Amenhotep readily learned the role of a king. Each day people came to the palace to have their arguments settled. Amenhotep settled more and more of these disputes with patience, good sense, and fairness. His father was pleased. The prince was wise beyond his years.

One day as I entered the throne room I knew something had changed. King Amenhotep III was nowhere to be seen. Then Queen Tiy

The new King—Amenhotep IV.

told me that he had decided to step down from the throne. His son, now called Amenhotep IV, was to be the sole ruler of Egypt. The year was 1369 B.C.

The coronation of a king was an elaborate and solemn occasion. It was held in the Temple of Amon. The incense was so thick you could see it. First, the priests of Amon, dressed in white robes and leopard skins, entered carrying the golden statue of Amon. My father, Aye, was among them. Then the old King and the new King came into view. I couldn't take my eyes off Amenhotep.

The new King was dressed from head to foot in gold. He even wore a gold beard. At the end of the ceremony, his father placed the crown on his head and kissed his cheek. *Amenhotep IV was now king.* As they moved to the palace, you could hear the people of Thebes shouting, "Long live the King! Long live the King!" All Egypt celebrated for days.

One evening my father entered my chamber and told me that the King wanted to see me. Aye looked happy but said no more. When we entered the palace, Amenhotep IV was seated on his throne. Standing nearby were his parents

When Amenhotep IV and I were married, royal portraits were made.

and my mother. King Amenhotep IV looked over to me and smiled. He told me that he had just been reading the writing on the holy stone from his parent's wedding. It said: "Amenhotep, son of the Sun, ruler of Thebes, living eternally, and the King's great wife Tiy, the immortal."

Amenhotep IV had decided to marry. I, Nefertiti, was his choice. Believe it or not, Amenhotep IV was just 16, and I was only 15!

We were married in the Temple of Amon. The ceremony lasted several days, but it seemed a short time to me. We were entertained with dancing, singing, and much feasting. The rich and powerful toasted us with wine. We could hear the people in the streets singing, "May your marriage last a million, million years." For the second time in a row, a king was marrying a commoner. *Hathor*, the goddess of love and joy, had been most kind to me. I was grateful and so happy. *Little did I know what fate awaited me!*

In the months that followed, we sat proudly on our thrones. I had trouble remembering we were not only royalty now; we were also like gods. To the people of Egypt, we had become divine.

Chapter 5

TROUBLE AHEAD

During this time, Amenhotep IV became very interested in religion. He spent hours discussing the role of the gods with Aye. He wanted to know more about *Re,* a sun god. Amenhotep began to worry the important members of his court. He had odd ideas for a king. Why was he interested in sun worship through a new god and not in Amon? Then Amenhotep announced that he now believed the supreme god was not Amon at all, but a god named *Aton*—the sun itself. *This new belief got us all into a lot of trouble.*

The more the King talked, the more I believed he might be right—Aton, not Amon, could be the most powerful of the gods. You can imagine how the priests of Amon started to worry. The priests knew that this new thinking might be their end. They tried to discourage the King but couldn't. They even tried to convince me, but I agreed with Amenhotep because I knew his secret. He told me why he believed in the new god.

Amenhotep IV wanted a sign from the gods. One night he went to the Temple of Amon. He stood in front of the statue of Amon. Nothing happened. He returned and spent a sleepless night, wondering why a new king would not have a message from the most powerful of the Egyptian gods.

Amenhotep woke me just before dawn. We walked out onto the balcony. Only a few guards were on duty. The city was still deep in sleep. Then in the east, the edge of the sun came into view. The sun seemed to be the only thing in all the world, other than us. Amenhotep was very excited. It was the sign. He was sure. Aton, the sun itself, was the true god of kings. He took my hand in his and said, "Nefertiti, now that I am King, many things will change." Amenhotep later wrote of this new feeling:

Thou appearest beautifully on
the horizon of heaven,
Thou living Aton, the beginning of life!

Amenhotep IV ordered that a Temple of Aton be built at Karnak. The priests of Amon didn't like it. They said it would upset the way things were. But Amenhotep IV commanded that the city of Thebes be known as "No-Aton, the City of Aton."

Amenhotep IV changed his name from Amenhotep ("Amon Is Satisfied") to *Akhenaton* ("He Who Is Beneficial to Aton"). He gave me the name of *Neferneferuaton* ("Beautiful Is the Beauty of Aton"). The priests were beside themselves. This was the final insult.

I tried to reason with the priests. After all, what was the difference between Amon and Aton? One was the sun god. The other was the sun itself. "The difference," I said, "is small." But I knew it wasn't. The King was saying that Aton was the one true god, *the only god.*

For centuries, the Egyptians had been worshipping *hundreds* of gods. Even the crocodile was holy to us. The priests knew that if there were only one god, everything the Egyptians had believed was now open to question.

My husband went even further. Akhenaton was upset. Just building a temple for Aton at Karnak wasn't good enough. Every important god had a special place. Karnak was located in Thebes and Amon was already the god of Thebes. Memphis had Sekhmet, a woman with the head of a lion. Akhenaton wanted the same for Aton—a special place that belonged only to this god. The King left by chariot with some new priests of Aton to search for just such a place.

Giant statues lined the Avenue of the Sphinx at Karnak.

There are stories that he drove his golden chariot until the sun was directly overhead. And then he stopped. But I know that Akhenaton chose the place because it was so beautiful. It was bounded on one side by the Nile and on the other side by cliffs.

There he drove wood stakes to mark the place where the new city—Akhetaton—would stand. On one of the stakes, he wrote, "I have made Akhetaton for my father, Aton, forever and ever."

And a good omen soon appeared. We had a baby—a beautiful baby girl. We named her Meritaton ("Beloved of Aton").

Akhenaton drove his golden chariot to find a place to build the city of Akhetaton.

Chapter 6

AKHETATON

Akhenaton returned to Thebes bursting with ideas for his new city. He chose a man named Bek to be his royal architect. Together they drew up the plans. The city was to be two miles long and a half-mile wide. The first thing to be built was, of course, a temple for Aton. Next would come the Great Palace and then palaces for Akhenaton's family.

Through the center of the city would run the King's Highway. Akhetaton would be the first *planned* city in history.

It was the spring of 1368 B.C. We were busy with preparations for building the new city. Workers and supplies would have to be moved there. A fleet of barges was loaded with people and goods for the 240-mile trip down the Nile River. From his throne on the royal barge, Akhenaton announced: "Whoever has purpose with the King must come to Aton's city."

The busy port of Thebes was now still. Thebes was no longer the City of Kings. A city yet to be built down river was now the capital of Egypt. As the barges, under their colorful flags, drifted down the muddy river, the priests of Amon watched their power slowly slipping away. My father was the only cheerful priest in the city. Aye was now a priest of Aton.

When we arrived, a large town of tents was set up and work began immediately. Workers went off to the nearby cliffs to cut stone. Others cleared the land. From the shade of the royal tent, I watched the work with Meritaton and our second daughter, Meketaton ("Virtue of Aton"). The blocks were fitted together for the Temple of Aton.

"The House of the Sun," as it was often called, was a tremendous building a half-mile

Akhenaton and I made special offerings to our great god Aton.

These few stone blocks are all that remain of the once-great temple of Akhenaton at Karnak.

long, ringed with columns and filled with altars and tables for making offerings. When it was completed, Akhenaton and I led the people inside. We both made offerings to Aton and my name appeared alongside the King's on monuments. Meritaton shook a *sistrum* (the rattle used in religious ceremonies), and I placed lotus blossoms on the altar. Akhenaton led the people in prayer: "The living Aton, the lord of all that the sun encircles, he who illuminates Egypt, the lord of sunbeams."

Some time afterwards, the Great Palace was ready for us. The walls were made of dried blocks of mud from the Nile. They were painted with scenes of all that Aton shone upon. Everything in the palace—from a wall painting of an antelope to the sun-shaped mirrors—was fashioned by our artists.

When the royal family appeared at the "window of appearances," the crowds below greeted us. As the cheering faded, Akhenaton spoke: "Grant a great age to the Queen Nefertiti, long years may she keep the hand of the King. Grant a great age to the royal daughter Meritaton and to the royal daughter Meketaton and to their children; may they keep the hand of the Queen, their mother, forever."

Afterwards we all stood on the bridge between the Great Palace and the King's house and watched the many chariots below. To the south, men were already at work on a smaller temple, the "Mansion of the Aton." We crossed the bridge to the garden so that the princesses could play near the lake. They would try to catch bolti fish with their bare hands as their father and I had when we were children. It was a glorious day.

Another palace, the North Palace, was built especially for me. And off in the distance, our tombs were underway.

For the rich people of our city there were private estates. The workers too had houses. Everyone in Akhetaton had a place to live. It was the most beautiful city the world had ever seen. There may *never* be a more beautiful one.

There was even a special section of the city for the many artists who decorated every part of the city with their work. The most well-known of these artists was Tuthmose, who lived on the Street of Sculptors. He carved and molded statue after statue of royalty, the wealthy, and even the poor. I was particularly pleased with one he did of me and I gave him a lotus *amulet* (or charm) to bring him good luck and long life.

Our artists were given great new freedom. Before our time, artists showed kings as great military leaders and as gods on earth. Akhenaton didn't pretend to be either.

Our artists were allowed to show things as they really were. So there were portraits of Akhenaton that were not very flatttering—flat head, big belly, things like that. And they showed our family as we really were. We were a family who enjoyed each other and expressed affection. Akhenaton and I sitting on the same size stools. Our children, drawn not as small adults, but as children, with their loving parents.

Chapter 7

THE DEATH OF AMENHOTEP

In 1361 B.C., Amenhotep III, my husband's father, died. Akhenaton returned to Thebes. I stayed behind in Akhetaton to care for the princesses. We now had four beautiful daughters, but we were still hoping for a son. Akhenaton was very unhappy with me. He so wanted an heir to the throne.

It was sad to receive Akhenaton's messages about how Queen Tiy and the people of Thebes poured dust over their heads in their grief. He sent word to me that the priests of Amon were now openly enemies of their King. They hated our new city and our worship of Aton. Akhenaton even heard them discussing the time when a *true king* would once again rule the land from Thebes. I was a little afraid for Akhenaton's safety.

After the two months of mourning for his father, Akhenaton came back to his beloved city. While he was away, I had ordered a prayer carved in the stone of a nearby cliff: "Grant to thy son who loves thee, life and truth to the lord of the land, that he may live united with thee in eternity. As for his wife, the Queen Nefertiti, may she live forever eternally by his side, well pleasing to thee; she admires what thou hast created day by day."

Akhenaton was overjoyed to be back. Once again we turned to a life spent in the worship of Aton and the building of his holy city.

But the beginnings of bad fortune were upon us. Once started, our bad luck never ceased. Death visited us once again. Our daughter Meketaton died. The King and I suffered great grief. We buried Meketaton in the unfinished Royal Tomb. Even when we had two more children, the Princesses Baqtaton and Setepenaton, our grief lingered on.

The priests of Amon did not approve of Akhenaton's belief in only one god. They plotted to destroy Akhenaton's power.

Akhenaton, in his great sadness, could no longer allow the worship of the false god, Amon. He ordered the destruction of Amon's name all over Egypt. It was a dangerous thing to do. The priests of Amon called Akhenaton a traitor. I feared what the outcome of my husband's actions might be. We soon found out.

All over Egypt the priests of Amon were growing in strength. They were plotting against Akhenaton. The enemies of Egypt, upon hearing of this religious dispute, were growing bolder in their attacks on Egypt's lands. I warned Akhenaton of the danger. Even Aye, whom he had trusted throughout his life, was unable to persuade Akhenaton of the danger.

The people of Egypt did not side with Akhenaton. Even though he told them that the true way was to worship Aton, they wouldn't change. How, they asked, could one god take over for their hundreds of gods? They wanted another king—one like Akhenaton's father. They wanted a king who was a warrior and statesman, not a religious man. A revolution was growing in Egypt. I could *feel* it!

In 1359 B.C., Queen Tiy's body returned to Thebes on a funeral barge to join her husband in his tomb. It was a very sad time for us all.

In 1356 B.C., Akhenaton was only 29 years old. But already there were many who posed threats to his reign. My father and I warned Akhenaton of the many dangers to him and to Egypt. The Hittites were taking over lands formerly held by Egypt. Foreign kings sent messages to the "Lord of the Two Lands" beseeching him to "bring help, before it is too late." But the King ignored all warnings.

One day as we walked to the sunshade temples, we heard of the rebellion in the army. Soldiers were fighting with their officers. That night Aye talked to Akhenaton. He told him that Egypt was about to collapse.

Somehow the King would have to get back the confidence of the military and the priests of Amon. Akhenaton was very upset. "Does that mean," he asked, "that the royal city will be moved from Akhetaton to Thebes? Will Thebes once again be 'No-Amon,' the City of Amon?" The look in my father's eyes told him the answer he did not want to hear. Akhenaton said nothing. He just turned and walked slowly back to the Temple of Aton.

All around us I saw our world crumbling. One daughter was dead. Another daughter had moved far away to Babylonia where she married the prince. Our daughter, Meritaton, turned against her father and me. She went to Thebes, where the priests of Amon tried to make her the Queen of Egypt in my place.

The more troubled times became, the less Akhenaton was able to do anything about it. I remember his once saying that he wished he could have been a priest. That, he said, would have

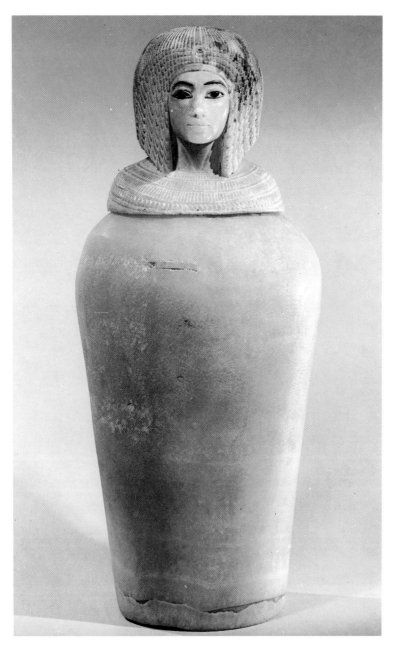

Our daughter Meritaton's head, as it was carved for the lid of a stone jar.

made him happy. He wanted to be left alone. He wanted to talk not with me but only his god Aton.

Not knowing what else to do, I left Akhenaton and went to live in the North Palace with my youngest daughter. When I got there, a lady-in-waiting told me that my daughter Meritaton's name had replaced mine in my own sunshade temple.

Chapter 8

The End

Years passed. It was 1353 B.C. Akhenaton finally came to live with me. It was heartbreaking to see him such a beaten man. None of his old enthusiasm remained. One afternoon he stood looking out to the fields. "All cattle are at peace in their pasture," he said. These were the last words I heard him speak. He died soon afterwards. He was only 32 years old when he was placed in his tomb. I made sure his long poem, "Hymn to Aton," was carved on the walls where he could read it:

> When thou settest in the west-
> ern horizon,
> Thy land is in darkness, in the
> manner of death.

Before the tomb was sealed, I placed a figure of a bolti fish next to him to remind him of the good days.

In 1352 B.C., I proclaimed a young boy of our city—Tutankhaton—King of Egypt. He would take my youngest daughter—Ankhesenaton—as his queen. They would have to move to Thebes to try to bring the country back together again. I would never again see my child or her husband, the King.

Aye also returned to Thebes and even took up the leopard skin of a priest of Amon. Once again, he became the Grand Vizier. With pressure from the priests of Amon, King Tutankhaton changed his name to Tutankhamon and Ankhesenaton changed her name to Ankhesenamon. Throughout Egypt the god Amon replaced Aton. Only in our city of Akhetaton was Aton worshipped.

The next eight years in Akhetaton were difficult ones. Barges no longer stopped at our docks and the King's Highway was deserted. There were no longer artists busy at work. Weeds, rather than flowers, grew in the parks. Almost everyone had returned to Thebes.

In 1344 B.C., young King Tutankhamon died. My father looked around for the next king. I was out of favor and unmarried. There were no male heirs. So, Aye chose himself to be king. His claim to the throne was that he was related to a queen. Certainly no one in Egypt was more qualified to be king.

The mask of the boy king, Tutankhamon, was discovered in his tomb in the Valley of the Kings.

Much of our life in ancient Egypt can be seen in the wall paintings in our tombs.

Just as he tried to keep alive our family rule, Aye tried to keep alive the memory of Akhenaton. As King, he added on to the Temple of Aton started by Akhenaton at Karnak so long ago. But by this time, Aye was old. He wouldn't be able to stay in power long.

I felt that there was only one thing to do. I wrote to the Hittite king, our archenemy, and asked if I or my daughter could marry one of his sons. It was a desperate move, but it seemed the only way to save the kingdom. A prince was sent, but he was killed by Harmhab's troops. Harmhab wanted the throne for himself.

My father died in 1342 B.C. After over 50 years of faithful service to four kings, my father, as King himself, was dead. He was buried in the Valley of the Kings.

A favorite of the priests of Amon, Harmhab, took over the throne. He tore down the Temple of Aton at Karnak and built two towers in front

Harmhab,
the commander-in-chief
of Tutankhamon's armies.

of the Temple of Amon. With the backing of the priests, he declared that he had actually been king since 1369 B.C.—as if Akhenaton, Tutankhamon, and Aye had never existed. *As if I, Nefertiti, had never lived.*

One afternoon a messenger ran up to me, bowed low, and told me that troops of Harmhab were on their way to wreck the city of Akhetaton. They had vowed to level it to the sands of the desert. After he left, I walked to the Temple of Aton. In the west, the sun was just fading over the Nile. "Oh, Aton, sun of the heavens and the earth. When thou settest in the western horizon, Thy land is in darkness in the manner of death."

Now I am dead these 3,000 years. Nothing more is known about me, about my husband, or my children. I went to my tomb with the secrets of my life . . . *and my death.* In the last years of my husband's life, he was angry with me. I couldn't produce a male heir. Not only that, I had begged his sworn enemy to marry me. Those last years of my life made me do things I will always regret.

In 1912, German archaeologists discovered the statue of Queen Nefertiti, Egypt's Queen of Mystery.

47

The tombs and mummies of Akhenaton and Nefertiti have never been found. It was once reported that a villager was seen carrying a golden coffin down a mountainside. Soon afterwards, jewelry bearing Nefertiti's name was being sold in local shops. But apparently, it is only a legend.

Perhaps someday someone will discover her tomb. And then the final chapter on Queen Nefertiti, Egypt's Queen of Mystery, can be written. Now we can only guess.

Was Nefertiti's walk to the temple her *last* walk? How did Nefertiti die? Was she killed by her own hand? Or was it at the hands of others? Was Nefertiti a religious traitor? These questions remain unanswered. But the search for Nefertiti continues.